In Somebody Else's Blood

Qiana M. Cutts

Cutts, Qiana
First edition

Cover design by Tiffany Stubbs
DezignDogma, dezigndogma.com

Author photo by Tiffany Stubbs
DezignerPhotos, dezignerphotos.smugmug.com

ISBN-13: 978-1544660516

Published in the United States of America.

If your love
is my darkest stain
I'll proudly wear
your mark,
for there is no
worse compromise
than neglection
of the heart.

*For the beautiful spirit who reminded me that love
is never a compromise.*

Contents

INTRODUCTION 1

I 4

   Order. 5
   Disclaimer. 6
   Discovery 7
   Word Speak. 8
   Fragmented. 9
   Untitled. 11
   Safe Space. 12
   The Life I'm Trying to Save is Mine. 13
   Engineers. 14
   Fearless. 15
   Gravity. 16

II 17

   Foresight. 18
   Hypothesis. 19
   Senior High. 20
   In Loco. 21
   Déjà vu. 22
   The Dance. 23
   Close to You. 24
   Muse. 25
   Dazed, in Circles. 27
   The Return. 28
   The Dance: Round 2. 29
   Touché. 30
   Surrender. 31
   Synergy. 32
   Naked. 33
   Sunshine. 35
   Reflexivity. 37
   Gone. 39
   The Dance: Round 3. 40
   Hardened. 41
   On Tuesday. 42

III 43
    Cherry Pickin. 44
    Genesis. 45
    Equation. 46
    Recollection. 47
    Medicine Woman. 48
    French Kiss. 49
    Beat Making. 50
    Climax. 51
    Transformation. 52
    Air Pocket. 53
    Mixed Messages. 54
    Deception. 55
    Past Due. 56
    Lashing [no. 1]. 57
    Tipping Point. 58
    Lashing [no. 2]. 59
    Refuge. 60
    Double Entendre. 61
    Longevity. 62
    Love's Resilience. 63

IV 64
    Vostok Station. 65
    Unrequited. 66
    Scorned. 67
    The Concession. 69
    Failure. 71
    Eclipse. 72
    Before and After. 73
    Straws Break My Back, Too. 74
    The Clay Was Molded Once. 75
    Solange Taught Me. 76
    Willpower. 77
    Savior. 78
    Salty. 79
    Communication. 80

V 81

A Thin Line..82

Lost. 83

Get the Weight Off. 85

Definition. 86

Sister.Girl.Friends – PostScript 87

Respect. 88

Alive. 89

Cycles. 90

Forever. 91

Selfless. 92

Reparation. 93

Post Affliction. 94

Lady Icarus. 95

Commodity. 96

Back to Reality. 97

INTRODUCTION

Audre Lorde's (1986) poem, "To the Poet Who Happens to be Black and the Black Poet Who Happens to be a Woman", became one of my favorite poems the first time I read it. The last stanza is especially striking. Lorde wrote:

> I cannot recall the words
> of my first poem
> but I remember a promise
> I made my pen
> never to leave it
> lying
> in somebody else's blood.

In 2016, I wrote these lines on a pink sticky note and posted the note next to the mirror in my bathroom. Lorde's words hung alongside affirmations, questions, song lyrics and other poets' words. I started writing the notes during a transitional period in my life. I had accepted a professional position and moved four hours away from the place that I called home for 13 years. I also was in the midst of some relationship challenges as I explored who I was, who I had become and who I wanted to be. I read each of the notes daily.

Initially, I interpreted Lorde's words as a message to writers: *Be responsible. Write without the intent to leave others pained.* I welcomed this responsibility and frequently thought about the impact of my words and the potential of leaving my pen lying in somebody else's blood. I wanted to write freely without conceding to the fear that my truth would be damaging to those enmeshed in my experiences.

The title for the first version of this book was *Hearts and Haikus.* Thankfully, I received feedback suggesting that I revise the title, as *Hearts and Haikus* did not do what good book titles must do: give a sense of what the writing is about and make the reader want to open and read the

1

book. For months, I thought about the title, the poems, and the experiences. I repeatedly asked myself, What is the book *really* about? Why would a reader want to open and read the book? For both questions, I had one answer – love. The poems are all about love and the ways it binds and shapes us. But still, I had no title.

My anxiety about a title increased and, on a particularly emotional day, I Netflix'd, cried, ate, slept and surmised that I had no title because the poems were not written well and no one would want to read them. That's how anxiety works. Also on that day, I received a random text from a friend that jolted my confidence. She texted, *You are amazing.* Another affirmation to add to the wall: *I AM amazing!* I added the note to the wall, and my eyes immediately were drawn to Lorde's words. Because I believe in signs from the Universe, I knew there was a reason her words drew me in at that vulnerable moment. It then occurred to me that leaving my pen lying in somebody else's blood is not only about being a responsible writer. It is about the ways I protect my heart or fail to do so and trust others will do the protecting for me. Leaving my pen lying in somebody else's blood is about the ways I love and have been loved. Epiphany. A title.

We enter this world covered and protected in somebody else's blood. But once we are here, we learn that we must define ourselves. We must curate our realities, fight our battles, and sometimes, leverage our hearts, all while internally desiring to be covered in and by somebody's blood. We want the safety of the blood but have no idea how to get back to that place. We spend our lives haphazardly looking for this safety. We take and give. We hurt and heal. We break hearts and are heart broken. We love and leave. Then we realize that we are again covered in somebody else's blood, either in the sense that we have pained someone so much we have taken his or her everything or we have given so much and have no more of ourselves left. But in those rare instances when love happens at the right time, in the right way, and with the right person, we are covered by somebody else's heart, thriving in his or her blood. I have been there and there and there.

This book is about love. It is about anyone who has experienced the various stages of love. It is about checking boxes, awkward dates, and "Good morning" texts. Introducing your love to your friends with, "Hey y'all. This is Bae." It is about laughter, multiple orgasms, and building. It is about that moment your juices flow – poetic or otherwise – when your fingertips touch Bae's. It is also about unrequited love, infidelity, and trust. Heated arguments and angry words. Fights in all the literal and figurative ways imaginable. It is about knowing when to walk away and being afraid to face the loneliness.

This book is not, however, a *whoa-is-me* book; so I hope you do not read it as such. Yes, there are poems where I grapple with feeling unloved. But there also are poems where I celebrate love, touch, and feeling. This is not a victim book. This is a *sometimes shit gets real* book. Because LOVE is never an all or nothing experience.

This book is about remaining in or getting back to that place where your first love is self-love, where the most important heart you explore is your own, where the comfort of somebody else's blood is secondary to the confidence of your tenderness.

This book is life in rhythm and lyrics. It is learning and progressing. It is understanding poetry is a necessity and knowing tears do not compromise strength, sadness does not defeat saving, and words have the power to transform.

This book is about growing through, getting lost in and healing from being *In Somebody Else's Blood.*

Thank you for opening and reading this book. I am humbled to have you experience love with me.

I

Learning who and why we are is difficult and necessary work.

Order.

I've been doing this all wrong
Loving myself in the end
with whatever emotion left
after the taking

It's hard to love
When exhaustion overwhelms

It's hard to love
When all I do is wax

About love

I ain't getting
I be needing

Wanting

So I write
Poems like this one
Have people thinking

> *This shit is sad.*
> *She needs to love herself better.*

As if they don't know this space
of doing what should have been

The first part

Last

Disclaimer.

Mama
taught me
how to love folks
who don't deserve it

Daddy
taught me
how to love folks
who are absent

I did

Discovery.

Some little girls play house
With other little girls
And like it

Don't let it phase
You

Word Speak.

I found my tongue
buried under lumps in my throat
hidden between cracks where
love tries desperately to peak through,
tucked behind shadows
of storm clouds that dance
with lightening bolts
before striking.

I found my tongue
lazy, limp and afraid,
numbed by pain and
unable to twist itself
into words that throw punches
with a desperate need to
connect.

I found my tongue
failing to rest at ease and
make room for screams to roll
over its horizon,
stuck to the roof of my mouth
guarded by sharp fangs
because insecurity
needs protection.

I found
my tongue

and

introduced it
to my pen.

Fragmented.

I be writing
myself whole.
Tryna counsel this
residual pain left
from moments when
rainbows are broken in
places that leave
room
for the sun
to shine through.

I be putting
words on pages with
loosed punctuation.
Stops and pauses
mean nothing on
a journey to
nowhere.
I'm going.

I be slanting
my rhymes
or leaving them
out,
altogether. When
connections made
are woven
with more than
the thread
of *-er* and *-ur*
next.

I be spitting
and reading
and performing
this work.
For life
is better lived
when scenes

of healing are heard
and visualized.
because someone
out there

Who be
writing.
Putting words.
Slanting rhymes.
Is still
in pieces of
self. Like
glass shards that
crackle under
calloused feets.

So I be writing.
myself from
fragmented
spaces.
In hopes that
we be
glued
and fixed
and sewed
together.

I be
writing.
We be
mending.

Untitled.

If Mama
hadn't made me
so independent
I'd know
some lovers
need to be
needed
more than they need
to be loved.

Safe Space.

Be gentle
with yourself
for the world
knows little softness
and places to rest
your heart safely
are few.

The Life I'm Trying to Save is Mine.

Poetry saves lives.
as words nurture tortured souls
and pack painful memories
in boxes nailed shut
with punctuation,
stanzas and rhymes.

Poetry saves lives.
when damaged spirits are
covered in imagined
and real scenarios
of resilience for
powerful it is,
to be a poet.

Who saves lives.

Engineers.

If we could write ourselves
in and out
of love,
we'd all be poets.

Fearless.

I know that Janie
left Eatonville
because
some places
ain't meant
for free women.

Gravity.

Women
always knew me better and deeper
Sisters and lovers
Who stood somewhere between
Holding me together
And ripping me to shreds
With no median

I made them beautiful
And they fell in love with me
For a time

I made them hate
And they paid me no attention
For a time

I spilled my tears
onto pages
Left bits and pieces
of my self-respect splattered
across their beds
screen-shotted on cell phones
saved to emails

But when it was good
Women
always knew me
Better
Deeper

II

*Remembering how the love made you feel is
balm for the mending.*

Foresight.

When love sets your soul
on fire,
make sure the
inhalation
doesn't kill you.

Hypothesis.

I wrote love letters to girls
from boys who didn't know
how to say, "I love you"
Who didn't know how to spell all the
dirty words in between

> I was 8, I think,
> But I knew how to use
> *pussy* correctly

I learned
that boys don't know how
to love
Unless there's pussy involved

> It was a theory
> That needed testing

I wrote love letters to boys
who said they loved me
claimed me in M.A.S.H.
put their arms around me at recess
walked me to class
carried my books

I did their homework
emotional labor
Gave them energy
kisses and
Pussy

Then they left

> Proof

Senior High.

We were love's graduation
with simple math
when
>1 +1 always equals
>One.
>Just. Us.

We solved problems
in transparent ways
for calculations
multipliers
and equations
of love are like

>past participles
>spliced commas

as the pause
is nowhere in sight

foreshadowing down unpaved
roads marching to

>metamorphosis

And at the end
of the journey
there's no history greater than

>"Do you love me? Yes □ or No □"

>*Check the Box.*

In Loco.

There was one
who knew how
to love
me

We were
synced like dope beats
sacred as the womb
rhythmic as poetic
lifelines

I'd ask, *Did you know...?*
and he'd respond, *I did.*
before I finished
as he was as much
in my head
as in my
soul

The deepest parts
of me
were his
playgrounds
transfusions
kryptonite

And when he came
to/in/for/with me
his eyes teared
caresses intensified
words mattered
and

> *I need you.*
> *I love you.*

Felt like forever

Déjà vu.

I must have lived in another body
Galaxies or generations away from this one
Because when we met
It wasn't the first time
I knew her from somewhere
I'd never seen her face
But her eyes were the same
Her heart as pure as I remember
Not remembering
Her touch as electric as fire
Not burning
And she knew me
And we sat with our knowing
Collected the memories
We couldn't recall
Touched with no knowledge of
Where we'd been
Who we'd been
Or how we got here
But we knew
Love

The Dance.

Foreplay/ed my heart
with gentle touches
to erogenous zones
that I didn't know existed
Kissed my spiritual awakening
and currents of passion
Energized my chakras
Opened my seven points of
awareness and I was
free to live and enamor

Her.

Loved
my quirkiness and
forced me to breathe
inhale only because
exhales release energies
that keep us connected

Taught
me that intersecting
journeys sometimes
keep moving
in different directions
in extended spaces
where the Universe
doesn't align

But not before She
mated with
my soul

and I Namaste/d
on the
sheets

Close to You.

When we hug, you connect with me internally
look into my eyes, then pull me
close to you
and your caress is the peaceful ocean I've needed
your touch, the only one I've ever really desired
and trusted

When we kiss, you hold each side of my face
look into my eyes, then pull me
close to you
and your lips are the softest I've ever felt
your tongue, the only one I've ever really wanted
in me

When we lust, you grab my left and right hip
look into my eyes, then pull me
close to you
and your strokes are the deepest I've ever accepted
your breasts, the only ones I've ever really touched
ravenously

When we argue, you capture all of my attention
look into my eyes, then pull me
close to you
and your words are the sharpest I've never wanted
your sentiments, the only ones I've ever really feared
breaking me

When we reconcile, you center my infatuation
look into my eyes, then pull me
close to you
and your apology is the quietest I've ever heard
your reluctance, the only thing I've ever really known
of you

Muse.

It's been a minute
since I've put paper to pen
or typed a few words
on this Microsoft Vista
because I ain't had no reason
to write or rhyme
been numb for a minute
but this is aaaaaa....
different feelin' I'm gettin
when I see your number
and face light up on that Blackberry screen
in mid-conversation with friends I'm like,
"My bad ya'll. I gotta take this call."
and I'm off in a corner
smile wide and eyes full beam
voice all soft and seductive
giggling with every line
you're feedin me

> you make me wanna write
> make me wanna put together
> some fly ass lines to spit at open mic

Take a deep breath before I begin
I'm nervous, palms all sweaty
and then
thoughts of our first meeting
as random as it was
I opened the door
you said "hello" and I fell in love
or maybe it was the pitcher
of sex on the beach
that had me feeling like there
could be
you and me
long conversations
passion-filled nights

you make me wanna write
make me wanna put together
some fly ass lines to spit at open mic

With my best figurative language
new metaphors and similes
been half-hearted for so long,
I wasn't sure if this could be
anything genuine, anything real
I'm not tryna be wifey, yet
just expressing how I feel

[eh-hem]

The voodoo that you do to me
is something kinda new to me.
I ain't used to being beautifully
swept off my feet

[deep breath]

and having no control
letting someone take hold
grab me by the reigns
picking my brain ~
or giving it
playing head games

[deep breath]

you make me wanna write
make me wanna put together
some fly ass lines to spit at open mic

Dazed, in Circles.

You discombobulate me
throw my mind into a whirlwind
of unobtainable dreams
caught in emotional limitations
can't end the confusion
or contain my enthusiasm
when speaking with you
about you

You bewilder me
got me standing in euphoria
writing good omelets
scrambling my words
hearing your voice
burrowing in
my brain

You unnerve me
challenge my calm to the nth degree
love mixed with fanaticism
weakened by your confidence
willing determination
to have me

You unearth me
get under my skin
conquered by all you bring
and take with
unrelenting desire

You love me
with an endearing restraint
that is
frightening as it is
intense

The Return.

Your love is
unexpected
forcing me to
reject it
I will
I won't
I do
I don't
love you back.

The Dance: Round 2.

We move in circles
dancing around all
that stares us in the face
We love uncomfortably
and pretend not to see
the signs
as they are there
prompting us to dance faster
move quickly
for neither of us has
the courage
the strength
the nerve
to say what needs to be said
So we dance
in, around, through
the circumstances
that brought us here
that keep us here
But at some point
the music stops
and we remain
our union is tested
No dancing to hide
what we know is true
through all the love
and all the passion
exists a space
a void
reminding us
that now
is not
our time

Touché.

She calmed the urges
for our bodies to fuse
and frolic to self-made
melodies

She annulled my power
to deny touch
I welcomed her
pleaded with her
fingers in

She took control
had me
panting and
biting my bottom lip
pulling sheets tighter
beneath muted moans

She smiled at my defeat
stripped of any game
willing casualty
to the same okie doke
that I used to run

Surrender.

I give up
and give in
to you
Conquer me
make me yours
no questioning
the passion
you have
The love I feel

I give up
and give in
to these nights
when I'm daydreaming
bout being
in your arms
in your presence
kissing, touching
you
gently

I give up
and give in
to my craving
I can't seem
to control, prevent it
from consuming
all the adoration
you have
in your eyes
when you look
at me

I give up
and give in

Synergy.

Words are few
When we're together

I've gotten too close
Love too hard
Become all that I don't want
To be

        Intimidated
        Vying
        Wondering

She's gotten too close
Loves too hard
Become all that she is
Manifested

        Nonchalant
        Protective
        Controlling

And the air is thick
I wait for permission to breathe
But
This anticipation
ain't individual
This wanton behavior
ain't singular

She started. We wanted.
This hypnotic foreplay
A baptism in bodies
When lovers for a night
Fucked control

Together

Naked.

You asked me to honest.
Asked me to say what I need from you,
What I want.

I want fairytales.
But not those with princesses who look nothing like me.
Not those with damsels who feign distress to be saved.
Nah, not those.
I want Black Love fairytales.

Stories to tell our children as we hang pictures from our
Juneteenth celebrations and trip to Ghana.
Like remember that time we started the Soul Train line
at the block party?
Got drunk at that Maze featuring Frankie Beverly
concert?

Stories that make us social media #RelationshipGoals
Because: after decades together, we still flirt and are
giddy at one another's presence.
Still practice newlywed intimacy and have eyes only for
the commitment we made,
a promise to love beyond death.

Stories bout how we lost connection but were always
in the same place at the same time.
How we knocked down cards stacked against us.
How we ain't loved nobody else harder than we love each
other.

Because that's the truth, ain't it?

Ain't nobody ever made me feel like you.
Ain't nobody ever been able to satisfy like you.
Ain't nobody ever made me turn away suitors who
wanted to love me like Buster Broadnax

And take me where I wanna go.
where I wanna go.

With you.

Black Love fairytales.
With you.

Lifetime.
With you.

Whatever.
Wherever.
With you.

I want Black Love fairytales.
With you.

Because
You asked me to honest.

Sunshine.

She was summer.
Standing at the hem of spring
vibrant sunshine
with soft breezes playing
under her linen skirt.
At times, hot and humid
but easily cooled by the
depths of chlorined, fresh waters
for shallow places couldn't
keep her stimulated.

She was summer.
Time flew liked winged
eagles when she was around
and laughter contagiously
walked with her,
up from her diaphragm
tickling her breasts and jumping
to anyone in her midst.
For her spirit brought with it
a sense of calm
and peaceful acceptance.

She was summer.
Free like temperatures
that started the day
with gusts of stifled wind
and ended with still
heat after perspiration
settled on her forehead
and traveled its way down
her nose – the salty taste
dripping to her lips.

She was summer.
Fun like cupped fire hydrants,
thumbed garden hoses
spraying happiness,
innocently serious like bicycle
gangs of children, dirt-faced
and smelling like outside.

She was summer.

Reflexivity.

In the tradition
of full disclosure
I'll open myself to you
put all those emotions
on the table
bring them
to the surface
and then wait
for your decision
my response
fully disclosed
and bare

But you must know
in the nature
of full disclosure
I have to tell you
my truth
Have to let you know

I breathe YOU

And I'm not ashamed
that in the middle
of the night
I sometimes call your
name and wait
for you to return the call

T - E - L - E - P - A - T - H - I - C - A - L - L - Y

Reliving how you
used to feel me
longing for your touch
wanting to be privileged
enough to devour the air
that you've released
You blow it out
and I take it in

savoring the flavor
of what has been
Keeping these memories
sacred in Oshun's box,
I'd open myself to you
again because

We live this life
now
and we love like this
once

Gone.

Truth be told
I'd roll her blunts
Wash, fold, iron and hang
All her clothes
Prepare her meals 8 days a week
Offer her my body 366 days a year
Clean the house obsessively, compulsively
Celebrate each birthday like a milestone
Get on her Mama's good side
Memorize her Grandmama's cookbook
Birth babies with her last name
Drink Flat Tummy Tea
Wear the tightest waist trainer
Become a Queer Black Yogi
Dress like an Instagram model
Take dance lessons from Maliah
Tease my fro, rock some braids, or
Get a custom lace-front with the best bundles
Learn to swim and speak multiple languages
Go bungee jumping and skydiving
And drink her bath water
Through a straw
Just to make sure I never let
Any taste of her be lost
In a drain

The Dance: Round 3.

And we're off
Racing
double-dutching through clouded spaces
never in the same place,
simultaneously
The seesaw rarely moves
in the same direction
one up, one down
that's how we groove,
but when the music stops
and the party's over
someone has to keep dancing
because that's the way we
keep it going
back
back, forth
and forth
and still in the same spot

we regress
we hurt
we love

and can't let go

Hardened.

He didn't want me
to love him

But he called
and he kissed
and he text
and he missed
and he caressed
and he sexed
and he held
and he vexed

and he entered me

So I loved him
because we did all the things
that lovers do

On Tuesday.

I
saw your face
in everyone who passed
mouthed our lyrics
when the radio taunted me
with our songs

I love me enough for the both of us.

wore that perfume
you like
checked your Facebook
and Instagram
careful not to double-tap

I always liked your hair styled that way.

read old text messages
verbatim'd our conversation
heard your voice clearly
as I scrolled through the call log

Facetime 1 hour, 8 minutes

sprawled your pictures
across the bed
and lay there
missing you

III

Appreciate love in its smallest forms.

Cherry Pickin.

I did not expect
To bleed on his mama's sheets
I was a woman

Genesis.

The day I met Love
I thanked God for such favor
We were the eighth pair

Equation.

I wanted to know
What passion kept Her awake
So I could be that

Recollection.

How was I to know
That Her skin would feel like home
I'd been there before

Medicine Woman.

Her fingers caressed
All of my tender places
No room for sadness

French Kiss.

I slipped Her some tongue
Lips pressed against Her woman
Tasting Her honey

Beat Making.

No music needed
To set the stage or the mood
I'll just screamed loudly

Climax.

My legs squeezed tightly
As She tried to take me there
I arrived on time

Transformation.

His love protected
Cocooned my soul through stages
Until I could fly

Air Pocket.

I was more than high
Beyond Cloud 9 to the Ex
And then turbulence

Mixed Messages.

She said, "Don't love me"
Then treated me like a queen
What sense does that make?

Deception.

She was transparent
Like opaque stockings
At midnight

Past Due.

When the friendship dies
And passion is a battle
We hold on tighter

Lashing [no. 1].

Hands over my mouth
A selfless and painful act
For Her protection

Tipping Point.

Strong women don't last
Keeping tears in solitude
Release or rupture

Lashing [no. 2].

And sometimes the pain
Is so deep that only a
Lashing will heal you

Refuge.

Never love someone
So much that there's no armor
To protect yourself

Double Entendre.

Too many of us
Know how to hurt and very
Few know how to heal

Longevity.

If we laugh more with
Our Love and danced in the rain
We'd conquer the storms

Love's Resilience.

I hate this process
of loving and ending up
Alone, once again.

IV

*Remembering how the hurt made you feel is
motivation for the growing.*

Vostok Station.

Not even the fiercest

winter, ground covered

in beautiful

Deadly

snow to Mask

the ice and freezing

temperatures,

Storms

and Darkness,

is colder

than you

Unrequited.

Days long
With uncertainty
Nights short
With sleep

Heart aches
With misery
Teardrops
On cheeks

Doubt thrives
With urgency
A sadness
That creeps

Love dies
With mystery
When not meant
To be

Scorned.

Women who are quiet
and calm are often those
whose fire burns
the hottest,
whose retribution
leaves an imprint
so deep that the soul
recognizes its presence
as a blemish long into
the Afterlife.

These are the women
These are the women
the women whose peace
is predicated on knowledge
that stirring their consciousness
into anger, pushing their hearts
to black spaces
is rectified only with
the Coming.

Not even the smudging of sage
can clear their energy.

Not even
the smudging
of sage.

These are the women
These are the women
the women whose love,
when pushed and pushed
over boundaries
to crazed expressions
of pain, has intercourse
with fury and orgasms with
insanity.

As repeating denied requests
for respect
was the foreplay.

These are the women
These are the women
whose tears scorch the rain.
The women whose stares
detonate bodies leaving organs
dripping from their hands.

These are the women
These are the women
who should never be crossed
lightly : intentionally, because
these women leave
their marks as omens
wrapped in prayed hands.

and
Not even
the smudging
of sage.

Can clear their hurt.

The Concession.

I watched my spirit
disintegrate into pieces of insecurity
as I prayed to strength goddesses
who lived dormant in me

I played the domestic
stirred my confidence
into docile main courses
served to you with red wine

I nurtured a peaceful home
arranged furniture with feng shui accuracy
cleaned every corner
scrubbed baseboards
removed every speck of dust

I harnessed my heart
denied smiles to attractive
strangers and past lovers
eased the chaos
that swarmed your mind

I avoided friends
buried happiness in
feigned compassion
when you spoke lies
I desperately needed to believe

I made excuses
when my hair broke from its follicles
grayed to ashes, cremation in progress
as my organs fought to stay alive
heart working harder
to combat the new weight

I wore loose clothing
to disguise the paunch
nurtured by tumors birthed
from microscopic tissues
swelled to mammoth fisted masses

I became a makeup artist
covering the inflammation
as there was nothing natural
about the pain

I kept tissues
to stop the hemorrhages
fleeing vessels in my nose
signs that my pressure was unstable
as the love you gave

I buried my energy
walked the hallways in zombied fashion
owned my limitations and
forgot my attributes

I was too much of everything
and not enough of anything

I didn't fit
I was too big
too bold
too brave

For you
Only for you

Failure.

This death
is sharp

discomfort
cutting like knives
through quebracho
at 12,000 feet
gasping for air
while tears flow and
congeal over corpses

Anxiety
Panic
Loss

Only distance
and time
can mend,
perhaps

Wandering
searching
for rest,
on the horizons
but rejuvenation
exists in bardo:
intermediate state

and that
makes it hard to sleep

Eclipse.

Constellations
fill my eyes when
you walk into the room,
but black holes
prevent light
and magnetism.

Before and After.

Remember when
you wanted me

in my rawest form

lusted silently
as I captured attention

daydreamed about me
as your partner

fantasized about me
as your lover

admired my intellect
and fierceness

watched me
ooze sensuality
and be Sunshine
mother
woman
and queen

Remember when
you thought
you loved me
thought
you could
handle me

as I was

Straws Break My Back, Too.

I believed you when you said

Relationships are work.
I PUT IN LONG HOURS.
OVERTIME.

We need to spend more time together.
I DECLINED INVITATIONS.
PLANNED OUTINGS.

You're too independent.
I FAKED DEPENDENCY.
STOPPED LISTENING TO WEBBIE.

You never really loved me.
I LOVED HARDER.
FUCKED WITH INTENSITY.

She's just a friend.
I IGNORED INFIDELITY.
REPEATEDLY.

All of this is your fault.
I ACCEPTED RESPONSIBILITY.
INTERNALIZED.

Don't ever call me again!
I WON'T.

The Clay Was Molded Once.

We are not the same.
Although we tout our Queendom
with similar ferocity,
our crowns don't sit parallel
to one another;
our conjuring isn't matched
when we call the spirits;
the meeting of our thighs
explodes differently –
gives life discordantly.
The softness of our lips and
tastes of our tongues
bear no resemblance,
provoke no contrasting fires –
one dim and easily muffled
and the other, beautifully
suffocating. Burning with
no assistance.
Our energies don't compete.
Don't share levels,
or commonalities.
Even the smell at the napes
of our necks, the peak of
our breasts intoxicate
uniquely.
For we are not the same.

And no amount of pretending,
eyes closed wishing, will
make us
be.

Solange Taught Me.

i tried to write it away
i tried to put some words on paper
i tried to cry it away
but the tears didn't make it safer

i went through a bottle of wineeeeee
thought a few glasses would numb me
i tried to dance it away
but the pain flowed like the Chari

i tried to feel some amazing
but racing thoughts kept coming
it made me feel crazy

i slept it away
i prayed it away
i walked it away

away, away, away, away, away, away

it's like
when love doesn't try
and the pieces are
wrapped up in a shroud

it's like
when love doesn't try
and the pieces are
wrapped up in a shroud

Willpower.

I hate you
for making me
love you
so much
that
I couldn't hate you
if I wanted to;
instead,
I hate me
for loving you
so much
that
I can't seem
to hate you
when I need to.

Savior.

I can no longer
love you
beyond your
Self

Salty.

Damage was real
Knowledge evolved
Scars healed
Bruises dissolved

Lesson learned
Never again
Karma burns
Death by pen

Communication.

We talked about words.

And I was open with you. Told you how words cut me deep. How I remembered things said to me more often than I remembered things done. I was open with you. Told you how, as a little girl, I always covered my ears when voices were loud with anger. How I ran into the other room, put on headphones and turned up the volume on the TV when adults bellowed. I knew there were bad words coming. I was open with you. Told you how even now, as a grown woman, I cry when someone says mean things to me, to others. How I hate to use the word "hate" and how no human's physical appearance is ever "ugly", maybe "unattractive" to some. Never ugly. But spirit and character can be. I was open with you. Told you I wanted conversations with kindness, even when we disagreed. How I hear nothing after scathing words are said. I was open with you. Told you I took a deep breath before I spoke. How I never wanted to use words that I could not rescind.

We talked about words.

But you were not open with me. Never told me that words were your weapon. How death rolled off your tongue with ease. I learned there were bad words coming. No headphones in sight. You were not open with me. Never told me that something in you excited when your words left me in tears. How there was some connection between the verbal beatings and a boiling hatred of me. You were not open with me. Never told me that slurs were stored in your cheeks. How, at any moment, you were armed and ready to fire. You were not open with me. Never told me that you took no deep breaths before you spoke. How using words that you could not rescind would contribute to my breaking.

We talked about words.

V

Nothing is gained from the experience if we don't heal.

A Thin Line.

Therapist keeps asking me
What I want to do now
And I want to wallow
In what I should have done
Then

Get it all over me
Layer upon layer of guilt
Beat myself into submission
Until I'm
Bruised
Bloody

Again, unrecognizable

But

At some point
I have to forgive
Others and
Myself

I'm ready

Lost.

I don't know
where to begin

Can't figure out
how to save
myself

Don't recall
who I was

Don't know
how I lived

and fear
and wonder

who I will be
when *we*
becomes *me*

I don't know
how to begin

Can't figure out
how to love
myself

Don't recall
being alone

Don't know
how I thrived

and fear
and wonder

who I will be
when *we*
becomes *me*

I don't know
where
how

to begin

Get the Weight Off.

She is heavy.
her body thick with
care taking
and giving selflessly
wearing a smile that hides
all exhaustion
and pain
responding to inquiries
of "Hey girl, how you?"
with facades of wellness,
"Oh, I'm alright.
I can't complain."
'cause complaining is
permissible (only) for the weak.

She is heavy.
her tears appearing
without invitation or
(obvious) reason
addicted to concealing
all that is not representative
of Superwoman -
the caped queen
who saved the day,
slayed the monsters,
and made dinner.

She is heavy.
ignoring warning signs
to live
her life
unapologetically.
to nurture and care for
and love
herself.

Definition.

Who are we,
if not love?

How
do we navigate life's
journeys,
if not through emotions?
with levels of
intensity that breathe energy
into our bodies, spirits.
passion.
and suffocation
as *to feel* becomes
too feeling.

Then, fences and walls erect
for, none of us wants to be
too much of
anything.

Especially love.

But without love,
who are we?

Girrrrrrrrrrl.
I didn't want to say anything
Because we grown
And grown women do
What want
Until we don't want to do it
Anymore
But I started to tell you
Like that one time when he
And then you asked him
He lied
And you knew he was lying
I didn't want to say anything
Because I saw it in your face
You wanted to believe
Wanted it to get better
But you knew it wouldn't
Always trying to save
Something, someone
Do all the heavy lifting
I didn't want to say anything
But each time you cried
I was mad as fuck
Because you didn't deserve that
He didn't deserve you
I didn't want to say anything
But I prayed for you
And when you were done
Like, really done
Chile, I said quiet 'bout time
Under my breath
Thanked God for bringing you back
And asked

You okay, Sis?
You okay, Sis?

You okay, Sis.

Respect.

More desired
Than love

It curates actions
Eliminates the need
For words
Its magnetism
Preserves

For who doesn't
Want a thing

More desired
Than love?

Alive.

we need to feel
more.

LOVE

in it's purest form

uncut
and raw
with giggles
soft touches on
the backs of our
hands.
necks.
inner thighs.

feel more.

LOVE

bodies touching.
hearts dancing
in rhythmic motion.
because
feeling more.

LOVE

is like.
feeling.

more.

Cycles.

Love is a powerful force
makes us do what we said we wouldn't
accept what we said we shouldn't
beat ourselves for giving in
and then do it again
when *the (next) one*
comes along

Forever.

Hearts work best
when they're not
hardened.
Be open to love
again.

Selfless.

Too busy not wanting
to realize
I was needing
what I was out here
giving

Too focused on loving
and caring,
when I
shoulda been out here
living

Reparation.

Love me beyond
the insecurity of
rejection.

Remind me of
the sincerity of a
first kiss.

For when love
has been seeped in
pain,
recovery
requires
reassurance.

Post Affliction.

If
After the scars heal
The bruises disappear
The hinges secure

If
After the damage subsides
The processing initiates
The forgiveness begins

If
After the fact
You are alive
There's always poetry

Lady Icarus.

Last night I flew
Across galaxies,
Swam through oceans
Deeper than infinity
Walked miles and miles
of Saturn's rings
Only to arrive at
The same place

Reality
Is no match for
Dreams when deferment
Tortures like a
Festering sore
Hanging in the night,
with scabs falling
From wounded
Skin

When there are no
Magic carpets around
To whisk me
Away
But I have my wings
Dusted, ready to
Fly

Hoping not to
Get too close
To the
Sun

Commodity.

A woman who knows
herself fully, whose confidence
is bound not by her complexity,
is the hardest woman to love –
if you're not ready.
For this type of woman knows
her worth, her value
and won't accept anything less
than what she gives.

Back to Reality.

Standing outside of myself
Shell of the woman I was

Meditations revealed me
Holding firm in my truth

Loving enough to know
I will not go down
like this

As my prototype was full of life.
She danced and she
laughed and she loved – purely.
Fiercely lived in freedom, she did.

And she has returned
to me

She brought gifts of
terminal self-love
Reminded me to never again
maneuver molded versions
of false perfectionism
when I was happy and secure
as I was

I am here
Resurrected

Made in the USA
Lexington, KY
19 January 2018